How to read  meanings

The simple way to master this powerful method of divination

Contents

Introduction

Tarot cards are surrounded by a lot of unnecessary waffle and mystique.

There. I've said it.

The simple reality is that many people want to learn how to use this powerful form of divination, but find themselves overwhelmed with all the information they find themselves bombarded with. Who has time to memorize 78 individual card meanings anyway? Why does it have to be so hard?

Actually, it doesn't.

Reading Tarot is very straightforward, and it doesn't need to involve rote learning all the different cards and their traditional meanings. In fact, the more you research Tarot, the more you discover that everyone has their own individual interpretation of the symbols anyway.

So why not put together YOUR own individual interpretation?

This is not a book that will give you a list of meanings to refer to every time you get your cards out. There's plenty of those types of books already. Nobody needs another one.

No, this book is different. It's practical, hands-on, and designed to get you working with your cards immediately, so you can interpret them right from the start without ever having to memorize a list of meanings.

Once you've worked through the exercises in this book, you'll have developed a personal relationship with the cards, one which is unique to you, and which will make your readings even more potent as a result.

If you'd like to take your relationship with the cards even further, you can head on over to www.masteringtarotwithoutbooks.com/guided-meditation and sign up to my mailing list. You'll receive Tarot lessons and gifts, all free, including a guided meditation to help you connect with the symbolism of the cards.

Now read on and take your first step on a journey into the Tarot, a journey that will take you to places you never could have imagined.

Blessings

Thea Faye

PS Having worked with the Tarot for decades, over that time, I've picked up ideas and techniques from a wide range of sources and cannot in all honesty remember all the people who've influenced me. If you feel you are due credit for any of the content within this book, please contact me at info@masteringtarotwithoutbooks.com and I shall rectify the situation immediately.

Chapter One:
Tarot Myths Busted

No one really knows where the Tarot originated, but lots of theories abound.

- It's an ancient Egyptian system of divination
- The Atlanteans were told about it by aliens
- It was part of traditional Kabbalah
- It was invented by Romany Gypsies
- It's part of a complex magical system designed to achieve spiritual enlightenment
- [Insert your own myth here]

The reality is that, although the origins of Tarot are shrouded in mystery, we do know a certain amount about it and it's surprisingly mundane.

The Tarot first appeared sometime between 1420-40 in Northern Italy. Any visitor to Italy will be struck by how much Renaissance Italians loved including symbolism in everything they do, and this new set of cards was no different. The precursor to our modern-day playing cards, Tarot, or *Tarocchi* as it was known back then, was originally used for card games, the divinatory aspect added in later, around the late 18th century.

That's it! No scary witchcraft or mysticism involved. It isn't related to any specific religion or tradition, so you can adapt it to your own personal spiritual practices or keep it as a tool, nothing more, nothing less. It works regardless of whether you have religious or spiritual beliefs or are totally atheist.

Despite this, several myths have grown up around Tarot and then insinuated themselves into our contemporary subconscious to the point that these myths alone are enough to put some people off going anywhere near a Tarot deck, which is a pity. It's one thing to decide you don't want to know about your future; it's quite another to decide you don't want to learn about Tarot because of some groundless superstition.

So, here's some of the most common Tarot myths and the reality behind them:

The Tarot is a tool of the devil/inherently evil

As we've already seen, Tarot cards evolved out of a simple game. Nothing evil there.

Tarot cards are printed pieces of card manufactured in a factory (unless you're lucky enough to have a very talented artist friend who can make some for you). Now, we can argue about the evils of industry, but that doesn't make the cards themselves a good or bad thing. They just are.

Any evil you may find in them comes from the reader's intention, not the cards.

You must never buy your own Tarot cards

Utter nonsense! I'm not sure why it would matter who bought your cards, but although my mother bought my first deck for me, I purchased the Rider Waite deck I still use today, and it's always served me well.

While it's nice to have someone buy you a gift, choosing your own cards has the added advantage that you can select the deck that speaks to you. However you came about your cards, it won't make any difference to the accuracy of your readings.

You must never let anyone else use or touch your cards

If this one was true, it would be difficult for anyone to have a reading. I always get my clients to shuffle the cards if I'm doing an in-person reading, since I feel it gives better results.

Sure, it's good to show respect for your tools, so you might not want to let a toddler with jam-streaked fingers rifle through your cards, but the reality is it doesn't matter how many people handle your cards. They'll still work.

You must store your Tarot cards in silk

No, you don't. You can store them however you like. Keeping them wrapped up in something beautiful creates a good impression for your clients, but it doesn't impact on the accuracy of your readings.

You must be psychic to read Tarot cards

While working with the Tarot can help you develop your psychic abilities, you don't need any innate abilities to interpret the cards. You're working with archetypal symbols that speak to our deepest subconscious. Your talent as a Tarot reader comes down to your connection with the images rather than any additional psychism. The cards will tell you everything you need to know. Stick with what you see in the symbols and you won't go far wrong.

Tarot readings are 100% accurate

Aside from the fact that it's illegal to make claims of accuracy without proof, Tarot readers sometimes get things wrong. Even the best readers make mistakes.

A Tarot reading is a little like looking down the road you're currently traveling. If you like your current destination, great! Keep going! If not, change what you're doing to go somewhere else. The whole point of a Tarot reading is to get advice on the best way forward, which might mean changing what you're doing. Once you've switched your course, you've automatically invalidated your reading, which means its predictions may not come true now.

Tarot readings must always be carried out in person

While I personally prefer to do a reading for my clients in person, it really isn't necessary. You can do phone readings and internet readings and they'll still be just as accurate. The only difference is that you'll have to shuffle the cards on behalf of your client. That's it.

The Death card is a bad omen

It's natural to feel afraid when you get the Death card, but there are far more ominous cards in the deck. The Death card is more about change, the ending of one situation as a new one begins. Death is a natural part of the life cycle, clearing the way for something positive to develop.

While it's true that you could potentially read someone's death in the cards, it's highly unlikely, and even if it did come up, the Death card wouldn't tell you about it.

So, there you have it! A basic history of the Tarot alongside a few myths that should have been consigned to the history books a long time ago.

Chapter Two:
Choosing a Deck

My mother bought me my first deck of Tarot cards when I was 14, the Tarot of the Witches. Although I was fascinated by the images, which had been featured in the James Bond film, *Live and Let Die,* I struggled to connect with them and never had much luck reading the deck.

Seeing my lack of success, my mother bought me an art nouveau deck of cards. Although they were stunning, again, I couldn't interpret the images, which followed a story created by the artist, Matt Myers. While I could see it made sense, I simply couldn't remember someone else's vision, so my mother bought me yet another deck, the Celtic Tarot.

Finally, I had a deck that spoke to me and I was able to start doing readings. However, much as I loved my Celtic cards, I was never able to take the final leap to doing intuitive readings and always had to refer to the book to check what a card meant.

Fast forward a few years and I bought myself a Rider Waite deck. This was the final piece in the puzzle. At last, I could do readings without having to constantly refer to a book, *and* I'd put paid to the myth that cards will only work if someone else gifts them to you.

So, what's the point of this story?

Not all decks are created equal. Set yourself up for success and make it easy for you to read the cards.

Personally, there are only two decks I recommend to people: Rider Waite and Thoth. Most people get on very well with the Rider Waite or are deterred by the fact that the Thoth deck was created by Aleister Crowley and stick with that deck, but for those who don't connect with the Rider Waite imagery, Thoth tends to work exceptionally well.

The reason why I recommend these decks is that they were both designed by people with a strong understanding of the importance of symbols and the significance of particular images, right down to the colors used. Every single card in both the Major and Minor Arcana is crammed with meaningful imagery, which makes it very easy to interpret them at a glance. In addition, there are many good text- and workbooks available for both the Rider Waite and Thoth, so if you decide you want to research them, there's plenty of material to choose from.

Do you have to confine yourself to these two decks?

Of course not. If you *really* don't like either of them, feel free to work with another that appeals to you more. However, if you're going to go down this route, don't be seduced by pretty pictures. I'll be the first to admit that my beloved Rider Waite isn't exactly stunning. If I was going to choose a deck based on its looks, I'd be using my art nouveau cards. (They really are gorgeous.)

But as the saying goes, beauty is only skin deep. If you want to be able to give accurate, detailed readings, you need a deck that will give you accurate, detailed results, and it's much harder to do that with cards that have been produced with an emphasis on aesthetics over meaning.

At the very least, choose a deck that has purposeful symbolism in the Minor Arcana. Many decks focus on the archetypes of the Major Arcana, rendering the Minor Arcana as little more than an extended version of playing cards with four, instead of three, court cards. Unless you want to spend hours and hours memorizing what each of those 56 cards mean

– because that'll be the only way you'll be able to start interpreting them – use a deck that gives you visual clues to what a card represents.

If you've decided that you really don't want to use Rider Waite or Thoth, it's well worth making a trip to a local store that sells Tarot cards. They should have sample decks available for you to browse.

Take as long as you need to get a feel for each deck. Is there one that particularly grabs your attention? Remember – look deeper than superficial, pretty pictures. Be honest with yourself. Could you look at a card and be able to know what it means just by interpreting the images? Are the pictures ultimately rather basic or do they include little clues to what might be going on in your client's life?

If, after all of that, you decide you still want to go for the prettiest cards, then be my guest. Just don't be surprised if you find yourself going back to the store to buy yourself Rider Waite further down the line.

One final little note on decks. Some people love to hoard Tarot decks and who can blame them? There is some stunning artwork out there. I've heard people say that working with different decks makes it easier for them to explore the card meanings and maybe that approach will work for you.

However, I will say that it's an expensive way of getting to grips with your craft when selecting one powerful deck will yield excellent results and much faster.

Personally, I'd advise starting with a good deck and mastering that one first before moving on to another. Keep your focus clear and sharp and you may find that you lose the urge to buy more cards. And if you do decide to add to your Tarot collection, you'll find it so much easier to hit the ground running with new decks.

Chapter Three:
Your Tarot Journal

You should keep a Tarot journal when you begin working with the cards. You could use a notebook, but I'd recommend you get a ring binder instead. This will enable you to sort your notes in differing ways to suit your changing needs as your understanding develops. This way, you can add to sections, remove outdated information (although personally, I like to keep records of everything, even when I've got something wrong, as a reminder to myself of how far I've come), reorganize your notes, and build up an invaluable record of what the cards mean to you.

Ideally, you'll be working with the cards on a daily basis. In the rest of this book, I detail several different exercises designed to help you develop your own interpretations of the card. Some of these are most effective when you practice them every day; others work better if you return to them once a week. Make time in your schedule for Tarot study daily. Even five minutes will start to make a big difference in very short time.

After all, the best way to learn Tarot is to work with the cards. Book learning is great, and you can pick up a lot from experienced authors, but if you want to be able to do readings *without* books as soon as possible, you can really only do that with practical, hands-on experience.

So now you've got your own deck of Tarot cards and your diary, let's get started!

Chapter Four:
Daily Card Exercise

Every morning take a moment to sit with your cards. Hold them in your hands, connecting with their energy, and when you're ready, choose one to work with that day.

You can do this in numerical order, starting with the Fool in the Major Arcana, working through to the World and then onto the Minor Arcana until you've worked with every card in the deck.

If this is what you choose to do, ask the card how can you help me today? What energies will you bring to my day? What are the lessons you can teach me or warnings you bring?

Make a note of your thoughts on the card. In the evening, write up how you feel it affected your day. If it didn't do anything, that's okay – write that down too. The more you think about the cards and attune yourself to their influence, the easier it will be to tap into their meaning.

Alternatively, choose a card at random. As you shuffle the cards, ask them a question like "What will my day be like?" or "What do I need to know about today?" Record your prediction and then at the end of the day, note how accurate you were.

Over time, you should find you become better at knowing what your day will be like. You'll learn what you can do to avoid any difficult situations that arise or how you can make the most of opportunities coming your way.

Whichever method you choose, when you go to bed, sleep with your chosen card under your pillow. Again, diarize any strange dreams you may have or any messages you get during the night.

This is a very simple daily exercise, but it is surprisingly powerful. However, you can take it a step further.

You'll need to set aside around 15 minutes to work with your daily card. It is entirely up to you whether you choose to do this at the start of the day as part of your prediction or at a more convenient time. Whenever you decide to do this exercise, try to stick to the same time each day so you get into a routine.

Ideally, you want to leave 24 hours between cards to give yourself time to digest and assimilate the meaning of the card. It also helps you to keep the cards individually in your mind, so you don't confuse them with one another.

Find somewhere quiet to sit with your card. Now, just look at it for around a minute. Write down in your diary your initial reactions to it. Think about:

- What jumped out at you when you first looked at the card? Did anything strike you as particularly important?
- Did you have an emotional reaction to the card? What?
- Does the card strike you as positive or negative? Neutral?
- How would you describe the feeling conveyed by the card?
- Who is in the card?
- What are they doing?
- What does the scene depict?
- What is happening in the background?

Once you've finished documenting your thoughts, it's time to examine the card in more detail. Write out a detailed description of what you can see.

- What colors are used? Does any color dominate? How does this affect the mood?
- What people are in the card, if any? What are they wearing? What are they doing? How are they feeling?

- What animals are in the card, if any? What significance does that animal have for you?
- What is the weather like? Where is the sun in the sky, if it's there?

Write down everything you can see and what associations you have with the symbols. You may find your description of a card changes over time as you notice new things. It may be that when a card comes up in a reading, different things strike you as important about it with different clients because those are the messages that they need to hear.

Studying the Tarot is an ongoing process – after 30 years, I'm still discovering new things about the cards.

Don't limit or restrict yourself. Just let your thoughts flow out onto the paper. Don't worry about getting the same results as other people – this is about *your* personal relationship with the cards, so there are no right or wrong answers. Only your connection with the card.

This process will help you start interpreting the cards without you even realizing it. You'll start to develop an intuitive understanding of what the cards mean for you, which you can then apply to your clients. What's more, you'll build up your own reference book that you can turn to when you're not sure what a card might mean, which is invaluable – and far more useful than letting someone else dictate to you what the cards are about.

You can take these exercises even further by meditating with the cards. This allows you to connect with the imagery on a deeply personal level and reveal hidden messages you might not otherwise have noticed.

Chapter Five:
Minor Arcana

Now it's time to dig a little deeper into the Minor Arcana. The precursor to our modern-day playing cards, the Minor Arcana consists of four suits of 14 cards. Unlike the Jack, Queen, and King of a contemporary deck, each suit of the Minor Arcana has four court cards. These are usually known as the Page, Knight, Queen, and King, although some decks use different names, e.g. Prince, Princess, Queen, and King.

These are my associations with the different suits and their numbers. If you find that the cards mean something else to you, follow your own instincts.

The Wands

The Wands, or Batons as they're sometimes known, are associated with fire. Wands cards deal with action, inspiration and change for the better. Negatives can include vanity, aggression and an inflated ego.

The Cups

Unsurprisingly, Cups are associated with water. This means they're associated with love, relationships, intuition and emotions. Negatives can be uncontrolled emotion, sadness and depression.

The Swords

The Swords suit is associated with air. It deals with intellect, communication and intellectual knowledge. Negatives of swords include pessimism, manipulation and mental unrest.

The Pentacles

Pentacles are sometimes called coins and are associated with earth. They tell you about finances, work, health and the material world. Negatives can include stubbornness, greed and miserliness.

Now that you have a basic idea of what the four suits mean, it's time to connect that to the numbers of each card:

1. New beginnings
2. Partnerships and decisions
3. Development of plans
4. Stability and consolidation
5. Disappointment and change
6. Success

7. Illusion and the realization that a new approach is necessary
8. Hard effort and strength
9. Possibilities and a pause before committing to a goal
10. Completion of the matter

Page: An immature person/project or child/project in its infancy
Knight: A young person (in their twenties)/relatively new project
Queen: A more mature woman/mature project
King: A mature man/fully realized project

All that's left to do is to cross reference the suit to the card number and you're done!

So, for example, the ace of coins would indicate a new job or job offer, while the four of coins would suggest that financially you're in a stable position. See how simple this is?

Exercise

Now it's time to get a little more familiar with the Minor Arcana.

Separate out the court cards. Now see if you can match each court card to someone you know. As a starting point, you might like to use astrological signs to match up the cards:

Fire/Wands signs: Aries, Leo, Sagittarius

Water/Cups signs: Cancer, Scorpio, Pisces

Air/Swords signs: Gemini, Libra, Aquarius

Earth/Pentacles signs: Taurus, Virgo, Capricorn

Now take it a step further. Spread out ALL the Minor Arcana signs and see if you can match some of them up to people you know. Do you have a friend who just started a new relationship? Their card might be the Ace of Cups. A friend who is comfortably wealthy? They could be the ten of Pentacles. Someone who worries a lot? They might be the nine of Swords.

Or maybe you might like to connect the Minor Arcana to different experiences in your life. Maybe you started as a Page of Cups because you were an emotional child. As a teen, you were a Page of Swords because you were studying so hard. At college, you became the Three of Cups because you made some good friends, and so on and so on.

The more you start connecting cards to people's individual situations, the more you'll start to get a feel for what each card represents.

Chapter Six:
Major Arcana

Now we move on to the Major Arcana. This is a series of 22 archetypes, following the Fool's progression from his start as an innocent, throwing himself out into the arms of the universe and trusting it to catch him to becoming a complete, fully actualized, spiritually enlightened being.

The Major Arcana can be a little trickier to get a handle on than the Minor. There's no convenient cross-referencing system you can use and while there are various associations with each card, we're meant to be moving away from masses of memorization, remember?

So, what can we do to develop a connection with the Major Arcana?

Go on your own journey of discovery. Start with the Fool. What can you see on the card? A young man about to step off the edge of a cliff, a little dog at his heels, his worldly possessions packed into a handkerchief carried over his shoulder. Where might he be going? What might be motivating him to do such a thing?

Imagine you've met him. What would he say to you?

Once you've decided on what's happening to your Fool, move on to the next card, the Magician. What is the Magician doing? What might he want to tell you? Does he have something to teach you?

Once you've imagined an encounter with the Magician, we move onto the next card, the High Priestess. What is she doing? What does she have to say to you? What wisdom might she share with you as you progress along the Fool's path towards spiritual enlightenment?

And so on, and so on. With each card, think about what might happen and what they might have to offer you to help you create the World of his dreams.

Go through this process a few times. With each retelling of the story, you'll notice different aspects of the card and think about different things the characters and situations might have to offer. It won't take long before you'll be able to relate these encounters to your client's questions and circumstances.

Chapter Seven:
The Story of the Tarot

Now we're going to take the storytelling even further. You're going to use the entire deck to tell a story, and you're going to do this a few times.

Decide in advance how many cards you want to use and what each card is going to represent. So, let's say for example that you're going to use ten cards. Here's what your outline might look like:

1. This card gives you the hero of your story
2. Something unexpected happens to your hero
3. This is their reaction to the event
4. Now an obstacle appears
5. This is how they cope with the obstacle
6. They receive some bad news
7. This is their reaction to the news
8. They meet someone
9. This new character gives them an important message
10. Your hero has learned something from their adventures

Or here's another possible outline:

1. This gives you the setting for your story
2. This gives you the hero of your story
3. This is your hero's biggest strength
4. This is your hero's biggest weakness
5. This is a challenge they must face
6. This is someone/thing who helps them with their challenge
7. This is an unexpected setback
8. This is the solution to their setback...
9. ...which leads to another problem
10. This is the resolution to the story

You don't have to use ten cards. You might decide to do a simple 3 or 5 card story to get the feel for Tarot storytelling. The main point is to decide in advance what your outline would be and then use the cards to follow that outline.

Here's an example:

1. This card gives you the hero of your story: The Hierophant

This story follows the leader of a religious organization. He is responsible for supporting new members joining the organization and makes sure everyone knows the rules they must follow. A very conventional person, he can be quite narrow-minded and rigid in his thinking. He just wants everyone to fit in and achieve their potential within the confines of his organization.

2. Something unexpected happens to your hero: Three of Cups

"Good news!" The Hierophant looked up as one of his followers burst into his chambers.

"What is it?" he asked.

"We have just learned that the aims that we had for the organization have been achieved! Everyone is celebrating together, rejoicing that we've been able to help our community and grow the organization."

"That *is* good news," replied the Hierophant. "And so much sooner than we expected."

3. This is their reaction to the event: Judgement

After dismissing his follower, the Hierophant was left alone to consider the news. He'd worked so hard to build the organization and make it successful. If anyone were to look at his life's work, they would surely be impressed. Yet now they had the membership and standing that he'd wanted for the group, he couldn't be completely satisfied. He realized that the work had only just begun. Maybe he wasn't the right person to lead the organization into this new phase of its development. Perhaps he should step aside and focus on his own spiritual growth and understanding. Was this his true calling?

4. Now an obstacle appears: Queen of Cups

As the Hierophant considered his next move, there was a knock at the door.

"Come in!" he called. He smiled when he saw Miranda walk in. The followers had dubbed her the Queen of Cups because she was one of the most nurturing, compassionate and caring people you could ever hope to meet. "What can I do for you?"

"It's more what I can do for you," Miranda replied. "I know things are going well for the organization, but I had the feeling that you were troubled."

"You're right," sighed the Hierophant. "You've always been so intuitive and caring and your instincts are spot on, as always.

I'm wondering whether I should continue to lead the organization."

"You need to trust your inner voice," Miranda advised. "Listen to what your gut is telling you. If you think you need to move on, then that's what you should do. But who will lead the organization in your place?"

The Hierophant paused to think. "What about you?" he asked. "You would be perfect to lead. Everyone loves you. They would be happy to do what you tell them to."

"Me?" Miranda laughed. "Oh no. I don't want to lead. You'll have to find someone else if you want to pass on the crown."

5. This is how they cope with the obstacle: Queen of Wands

Miranda walked out, leaving the Hierophant to think about who else he might ask to lead in his stead.

Then it hit him. "Of course! Elizabeth!"

Elizabeth had been dubbed the Queen of Wands because she was so energetic and busy. She was an inspiration to all around her and a natural leader. Many a time, he'd turned to Elizabeth for advice and been struck by her practical, go-getter approach that always made him feel as though he could achieve anything he wanted. Creative and optimistic, she was full of passion for the organization, and had the charisma to win over anyone who encountered her.

Yes, he would ask Elizabeth to take over. She was the perfect choice.

6. They receive some bad news: The Tower

Smiling to himself, the Hierophant started to write the official letter that would pass over leadership of the organization to Elizabeth. But he had barely written his first sentence when another one of his followers burst in.

"Yes?" sighed the Hierophant, trying to control his irritation. "What is it now?"

"Terrible news!" cried the follower. "The King has just announced that all religious organizations are to be disbanded. It will now be illegal for any religious organization to gather on pain of death. What are we to do?"

What could they do? It was one thing for the Hierophant to step down as leader, but he had never even considered not having anything to do with the organization. He had been part of it his whole life. He couldn't imagine a world without his organization.

And what about all the people who were members? They lived in the organization's buildings, worked for the organization, were fed by the organization. Where would they all go? What would they do?

7. This is their reaction to the news: Ace of Wands

The Hierophant did what he'd always done in crisis: sat down and thought through his options. Even the worst situation offered opportunities. There was a solution to every problem. He just had to consider what the best way forward would be.

He realized that this was a time of action. While the organization was a spiritual, peaceful group, they were not going to accept the King's orders without question. Before he even considered handing over leadership to someone, he had to solve this problem.

He was going to talk to the King.

8. They meet someone: 3 of Pentacles

The King was not in the best of moods when the Hierophant was granted audience with him.

"Yes? What do you want?" he snapped.

"I have come to talk to you about your decision to close all religious organizations." If the Hierophant was afraid, he didn't let it show. "I have worked all my life to develop an organization that is a credit to your kingdom, one built on strong foundations that can support your work. We have done lots of good work in the community and helped those in need. If you close our organization, many people will be in trouble. If we work together, we can make your kingdom even greater."

9. This new character gives them an important message: King of Wands

"I admire your passion," replied the King. "I like to set goals for myself, so I can understand your passion and will to make your organization even better. However, while I will remove the death penalty for those who join your organization, I would like you to consider changing the way you do things. While your community work is admirable, many of your members cloister themselves away from the world and focus on themselves to the exclusion of others. They have become stuck in their ways. I have even heard rumors of your wanting to step down as leader, so you can focus on yourself. Perhaps now is not the time. Instead, go out to the world. Show through your actions what can be achieved. Let your deeds stand as an example of what can be done. I know that you can be visionary in your thinking. The organization in its current form can no longer function, but I'm sure you'll come up with a creative solution that serves my kingdom better."

10. Your hero has learned something from their adventures: The Hermit

The Hierophant went away, lost in thought. Instead of returning to the organization, he went out into the countryside to take some time alone. The King was right. The organization did need to change.

And he needed to step down as leader.

Not because he wanted to focus on his personal spiritual development, but because, right now, a Wands person was needed at its head. Elizabeth would have the vision to create what the King wanted.

Meanwhile, the Hierophant needed to take some time to meditate and indulge in some introspection. He'd learned a lot during his time as leader. It was time to evaluate all those lessons. When he was ready, he would return to the organization and help Elizabeth. His new understandings would be able to support her in the next phase of the organization's development.

And there you have it! It's not the greatest piece of literature, but that's not the point. This exercise forces you to consider all the potential implications of a card and how they might be applied to real life situations.

When you write your own stories, don't worry about making them publishable. These are stories for your own personal journal. No one else ever has to see them. But these stories will take your understanding of the cards to a deeper level.

Chapter Eight:
Reading for Others

Now you have a strong understanding of the cards and what they might mean, it's time to prepare for doing readings for others.

It's very important to be aware of how your personal prejudices impact on your interpretations of the cards. It can be tempting sometimes to fall back on so-called cold reading, which is where you tell people what you think they want to hear or make guesses about them based on their appearance, your discussions, etc. You must keep your readings to what the cards tell you and ignore any assumptions you might make about your clients. After all, our prejudices and judgments about people can be wrong, but the cards will set us on the right path.

This is a great exercise to help you be aware of the need to be impartial. Be honest with yourself as you work through it – the more you can be self-aware, the better your readings will be.

Shuffle the cards while you consider the question *"What do I need to focus on right now?"*

Pull out one card. Now interpret it as if you were reading for the following people. Remember – ask yourself if you'd read it differently for different people and be honest with yourself about what prejudices would influence your reading:

- Yourself

- Your dad

- A sibling

- Someone you hate

- A 21-year-old man who recently graduated

- A 35-year-old woman who has just started a new business

- A 47-year-old man who has never had a serious relationship

- A 52-year-old woman with 2 children who recently married someone who also has 2 children

- A 64-year-old man whose wife is seriously ill in hospital

- A phone client you know absolutely nothing about

At the end of this exercise, you should have realized that it's virtually impossible to leave your own assumptions behind, which is fine. We're all human and part of what makes a good reader is our individual approach to the cards.

However, it is important to always come back to the cards to determine the answer to your client's questions. If the cards are telling you one thing but your head is telling you something else, *listen to the cards!*

If you are genuinely getting a strong feeling that your gut instinct overrides the usual interpretation of the cards, then tell your client. Say "This card would normally mean *x*, but I'm getting the feeling that right now it means *y*."

You owe it to your clients to be as honest as possible and to give them the message the cards have for them. Anything beyond that is a bonus – but there is always a risk when you pass on a message that is not based in the symbolism of the cards that it may simply be your ego speaking.

Be aware of this danger and always be ethical in your readings.

Chapter Nine:
Your Tarot Buddy

You can do as many exercises as you like and read every book ever published about Tarot, but the only way you're going to master the cards is with practice.

If you're feeling overwhelmed at the thought of reading for others, ease yourself into it gently. Find a Tarot buddy to work with. This can either be a friend who is happy for you to practice on them or, even better, someone who is learning to work with the cards themselves. If you can find a friend who is also interested at reading the cards, the pair of you can share your insights with each other and compare your personal interpretations to improve and refine your readings.

Start with single card readings. These are the simplest ways of reading the cards. You don't even have to go into detail. Ask a yes/no question while you shuffle the cards. Cut them, and if the card that comes up is the right way up, the answer is yes. If it's upside down, the answer is no. Simple as that!

Of course, you're going to want to do more than say yes or no, so take things a step further. Look at the card you've drawn and consider the symbolism and how it would relate to the question being asked.

For example, let's say you asked the question "Will I get a new job within the next two weeks?" You cut the cards and get the Sun, right way up. This is a resounding yes! Look further at the symbolism of the card. It's one of the Major Arcana, which suggests that this is an important new phase in your life, one which will have great significance for you. The sun shines down on a flourishing garden, suggesting that this will be a very prosperous job for you. A happy child carrying a pennant sits on a horse, suggesting that not only will you be very happy in this job, it's one that will take you to exciting new places in your life. Not necessarily physical places, but perhaps career opportunities you hadn't considered possible before.

Phew! That's a lot of information and it's only a one card reading!

As you practice your one card readings, you'll find yourself becoming more and more adept at understanding what the card is telling you at a glance. When you feel ready to start doing more involved spreads using more cards, you'll find it very easy to dive straight in because of all the groundwork you've already done.

Chapter Ten:
Conclusion

So, there you have it. Over the course of the previous few chapters, you've discovered several deceptively simple exercises that will enable you to start reading Tarot cards without ever needing to memorize a bunch of card meanings. Once you've finished working through them, you'll wonder why you ever thought it was necessary to stick to someone else's definition of what a card means when your own interpretations are much more powerful and will give you better, more accurate readings.

You'll find that as you start progressing through the exercises, you'll develop a momentum that will help you interpret cards you haven't studied yet. As you start to key in to the symbolism of your deck, you'll begin to intuitively know at a glance what each card should mean. Remember – practice is crucial, so see if you can expand your pool of willing volunteers who will be happy for you to do readings for them as you hone your skills until you feel completely confident in your abilities.

If you'd like to take your understanding of the cards even further, sign up to my Tarot mailing list at www.masteringtarotwithoutbooks.com/guided-meditation for free lessons, guided meditations and the occasional free gift.

Alternatively, email me at info@masteringtarotwithoutbooks.com if you have any questions. I'd be more than happy to help you progress on your path to working with this powerful tool.

Best of luck with your Tarot journey!

CPSIA information can be obtained
at www.ICGtesting.com
Printed in the USA
LVHW090807310721
694222LV00010B/118